WE WANT YOU TO WATCH

Alice Birch and RashDash

WE WANT YOU TO WATCH

Text: Alice Birch | Movement: RashDash

OBERON BOOKS
LONDON

WWW.OBERONBOOKS.COM

First published in 2015 by Oberon Books Ltd
521 Caledonian Road, London N7 9RH
Tel: +44 (0) 20 7607 3637 / Fax: +44 (0) 20 7607 3629
e-mail: info@oberonbooks.com
www.oberonbooks.com

A catalogue record for this book is available from the British
Library.

PB ISBN: 978-1-78319-925-9
E ISBN: 978-1-78319-926-6

Cover image designed by Graphic Design Studio
at National Theatre. Original photo © Getty Images

Printed, bound and converted
by CPI Group (UK) Ltd, Croydon, CR0 4YY.

Thanks to

Charlie Bennett

Ben Power

Caroline Steinbeis

Oli, Lloyd, Helena, Adam, Bettrys, Peter,
Laurence, Vicky, Becky, Alex, Max, Ben, Giles,
James, Heather, Sam and Arthur.

National Theatre

The National Theatre, where this play was presented in June 2015, is dedicated to making the very best theatre and sharing it with as many people as possible.

We stage up to 30 productions at our South Bank home each year, ranging from re-imagined classics – such as Greek tragedy and Shakespeare – to modern masterpieces and new work by contemporary writers and theatre-makers. The work we make strives to be as open, as diverse, as collaborative and as national as possible. We want to inspire artists and audiences to think in new ways, to constantly re-imagine the act of making theatre. Much of that new work is researched and developed at the NT Studio: we are committed to nurturing innovative work from new writers, directors, creative artists and performers.

The National's work is also seen on tour throughout the UK and internationally, and in collaborations and co-productions with regional theatres. Popular shows transfer to the West End and occasionally to Broadway; and through the National Theatre Live programme, we broadcast live performances to 1500 cinemas in 40 countries around the world.

Our extensive Learning programme offers talks, events and workshops for people of all ages in the new Clore Learning Centre, and reaches nationwide through programmes such as Connections, our annual festival of new plays for schools and youth theatres. From September, National Theatre: On Demand In Schools will make three acclaimed, curriculum-linked productions free to stream on demand in every secondary school in the country. Online, you'll find a rich variety of innovative digital content on every aspect of theatre.

We do all we can to keep ticket prices low and to reach a wide audience, and use our public funding to maintain artistic risk-taking, accessibility and diversity.

The National Theatre building first opened in 1976. Designed by architect Denys Lasdun, it houses three auditoriums: the Olivier, Lyttelton and Dorfman theatres. A fourth – temporary – theatre was added in 2013. Like a theatre factory, the building also houses departments skilled in making costumes, wigs, scenery, props and everything else required to bring productions to the stage.

Box Office and Information: +44(0) 20 7452 3000
National Theatre, South Bank, London SE1 9PX
nationaltheatre.org.uk
Registered Charity No: 224223

Director Rufus Norris
Executive Director Lisa Burger

We Want You To Watch was first performed at the temporary theatre, National Theatre, London on 11 June 2015 with the following cast:

PIG	*Abbi Greenland*
SISSY	*Helen Goalen*
THE OLD MAN	*Peter Marinker*
THE MEGA HACKER	*Bettrys Jones*
THE BEAUTIFUL MAN	*Lloyd Everitt*
THE QUEEN	*Helena Lymbery*
THE LITTLE BOY	*Adam Charteris*

Director	Caroline Steinbeis
Text	Alice Birch
Movement/Choreography	RashDash
Designer	Oliver Townsend
Lighting Director	Beky Stoddart
Music	Ben and Max Ringham
Sound Designer	Alex Caplen
Associate Director	Laurence Cook
Company Voice Work	Daniele Lydon
Casting	Charlotte Bevan
RashDash Producer	Charlotte Bennett
Production Manager	Marius Ronning
Stage Manager	John Fernandes
Deputy Stage Manager	Vicky Eames
Assistant Stage Manager	Surenee Chan Somchit
Costume Supervisor	Caroline McCall
Senior Technician	Jonathon Pascoe
Publicist	Susie Newbery
Production Photographer	Richard Davenport

Characters

PIG

SISSY

THE BEAUTIFUL MAN

THE QUEEN

THE LITTLE BOY

THE MEGA HACKER

THE OLD MAN

Note

/ Denotes the overlapping of speech.

Words in square brackets [ ] are not spoken.

The absence of a full stop at the end of a line denotes
a kind of interruption – the lines should run at speed.

The use of a full stop on a line on its own suggests
a pause – whether this is a single beat or ten minutes
depends on what feels right.

The spacing of the dialogue, the use of upper and lower case
letters and the punctuation is all there to help the actor in
terms of the pacing and the weight of their words.

The play has been co-authored by playwright Alice Birch, and theatre-makers and performers Abbi Greenland and Helen Goalen (RashDash).

The concept, characters and stories have been discovered and created collaboratively.

The verbal language and the movement languages are both equally important in the process of making and the presentation of this play. At points during the process the text has come first, and at points the movement/image has led.

We have a shared understanding between us that sometimes words are the best medium to articulate what we think and feel, and sometimes movement/image is.

It is difficult to record the movement world – which is movement and not words for very important reasons – with words. But we think it's important that the two exist alongside each other in this document.

The way we record the movement will change throughout the document. We want to capture why and how movement is articulate at each given moment. This isn't intended as a guide to how to do the original choreography – it has been made by and for each performer, and will always be its most articulate when it is so. It should be different for each new person that performs it.

Sometimes we will describe the processes we've used to embody and express the point/feeling/moment. Sometimes we will describe the pictures/movements, and the attitudes and intentions with which they're performed.

*embody – personify, give human form/shape to, realise, manifest, express, concretise, symbolise, represent, epitomise, encapsulate, typify, exemplify.

When we use the word **embody** we mean – show with your body or describe with your body.

– RashDash

1.

Low-hanging lights. Closed blinds. Early, about 5 a.m. PIG, SISSY
and THE BEAUTIFUL MAN.

THE BEAUTIFUL MAN has some blood on him.

A tape recorder is on the table.

It whirrs.

There is a symmetry to PIG and SISSY's
movement throughout this scene.
A kinship. They are a team.

SISSY	Would you like to start again?
MAN	I didn't do it
SISSY	Would you like to go from the top
MAN	I didn't do it
SISSY	Would you like to go back to the beginning
MAN	I didn't do it
PIG	See the thing is – the Thing is is that when you parrot I didn't do it At us then that makes it look a lot like you Did do it
MAN	I didn't I I I didn't – I didn't do it I
PIG	Why don't you tell us why you think you might be here
MAN	.
PIG	If you didn't do it, why might you be here?
SISSY	Where were you last Tuesday?
PIG	If you didn't do it, who did?
SISSY	Are you feeling okay
PIG	Your lips look a little blue, don't they look blue
SISSY	They do

11

PIG	You Sick Fuck
SISSY	Where were you last Tuesday
PIG	For the benefit of the tape, the suspect has just Stopped Talking
SISSY	Where were you last Tuesday
PIG	The suspect is making No response
SISSY	Where were you last Tuesday
PIG	The suspect continues to make No response
SISSY	Just in case anyone listening back to this thinks that the tape is broken or doesn't pick up your voice or something – perhaps a listener would begin to wonder whether your voice has a pitch that only Dogs can hear and you're talking and talking and we just can't Hear you perhaps any Auditor who happened upon the tape might assume that you're doing very expressive mime language and we're just failing to report that you should know that we can go for as long as you'd like to we have literally been here for thousands of years and I never use the word literally incorrectly I am a fucking pedant this can be your entire existence
MAN	I'd like I'd. I'd like to. I'd. I'd like to speak to my To my
SISSY	To your
MAN	To my
SISSY	To your
PIG	For the benefit of the tape
MAN	to my

PIG	That was the suspect's voice
MAN	I'd like to speak to my lawyer
SISSY	Okay
MAN	I have the right to a a a ph[one] a call a
SISSY	Okay
PIG	How're you Feeling
MAN	Look – my [family] will be worried
SISSY	Who will be worried
PIG	You seem to be sweating – is that a Cold Sweat
MAN	My – my – there will be People. People who who will be / worried
SISSY	/ Do you have a medical condition we ought to know about
PIG	Who will be worried
SISSY	Why don't you tell us a bit about that woman you chopped up into little pieces and left in an orchard for that dog walker to find
PIG	Why is it ALWAYS a dog walker it's always a fucking dog walker
SISSY	He had to pull a piece of that woman's Thigh out of his labrador's mouth can you Imagine how upsetting that must have been, I mean he must have been picking pieces of flesh out of his dog's teeth for days.

.

Perhaps PIG starts drinking at some point.

Perhaps SISSY starts smoking at some point.

MAN	I want to speak to my lawyer
PIG	I'm sure he's on his way

MAN	I didn't
SISSY	I'm sure she's just been held up
MAN	He's not a
PIG	Traffic can be hell, can't it
SISSY	This room can be difficult to find
PIG	Traffic can be a real fucking nightmare, can't it
SISSY	I'll make sure someone sends her some directions – could you send him some directions please?
PIG	I'll get right to it.
	.
SISSY	Where were you last Tuesday?
MAN	What
SISSY	Where were you, what were you doing Last Tuesday
MAN	I don't have to to [do this] I – .
	No comment
PIG	Don't do that, that is literally the stupidest thing you can do because I'll get pissed off and want to hurt your face again and your face is completely remarkable I want to lick it clean so I feel conflicted about causing it any more harm / CAN WE JUST SAY WE'RE COMPLETELY PRO SEX
SISSY	/ CAN WE JUST SAY WE'RE COMPLETELY PRO SEX where were you last Tuesday
MAN	No. No comment.
PIG	Was I not clear
SISSY	You were very clear
PIG	See now I thought I was clear

MAN   You c. You c. C. You c. C.

                PIG makes a noise a little like she is being strangled.

                .

PIG   Did you like that?

                Was this your first go?

                You went awfully big.

                I mean.

                You cut her face off. I mean. That's a step up from just
                wanking to all that rape porn.

                Isn't it?

                *SISSY pushes photographs of a dead woman whose
                body has been mutilated across the table.*

                The MAN stares.

SISSY   You were top of your class at school, weren't you

PIG   Actively involved in the debating and the drama clubs

SISSY   You listed Swimming, Food and Gardening as your list
                of Likes when you signed up to Facebook, didn't you

PIG   Two girlfriends at secondary school and three more
                since then

SISSY   You are consistently described as a Stand Up Guy

PIG   A Thoroughly decent individual you don't have the
                face of a killer, that's what the papers will say

SISSY   What happened then? You were a Good Guy – what
                changed

PIG   Why the sudden penchant – penchant is a good word
                – why the sudden Penchant for cutting up women and
                placing – I won't say dumping – because you absolutely
                Placed her in an allotment patch not far from the M26

SISSY   Was it something at home or a medical problem? Was it work? Had you had a sudden change at work? Were you promoted or demoted or

MAN   I'm a milkman

SISSY   Obviously we know that you're a milkman

PIG   What d'you think we Do here, of course we know that you're a milkman

MAN   I

PIG   Perhaps you were made Head MilkMan and there was a direct correlation between this promotion and your new-found enjoyment in suffocating women til their faces went blue. Perhaps there was a link between you suddenly being given the privilege of driving the Milk Float and discovering that removing a woman's breasts was to be your new favourite thing – or perhaps tying her wrists together, pushing your fingers up inside her rectum and punching causing her anus to prolapse no doubt causing immense pain before you'd barely got started was all because you had just been crowned the King of Dairy.

                .

MAN   That's ludicrous.

PIG   Correct.

SISSY opens a file of papers. She pulls out a huge sheet of paper.

SISSY   Where were you last Tuesday?

MAN   No comment

PIG makes him jump.

SISSY   I can tell you where you Weren't last Tuesday. You weren't in front of your computer. Which is noticeable. Given that you are Always in front of your computer.

PIG	You weren't at your computer because you were killing twenty-four-year-old dental student Laura Lahowderfisk
MAN	I didn't do it
SISSY	On Monday at 11.34 p.m. you watched Rape That Bitch Four three times in a row and on the fourth viewing you skipped to three minutes seventeen where they hold the woman down in a bath and bring her back up to catch her breath and rape her
PIG	Was that what you did – was that why it looked like you had washed her?
SISSY	She had several deep cuts on her breasts, identical to the women in Gag Me Then Fuck Me which you watched at 9.23 a.m. on the Tuesday morning
PIG	Did you watch it while you ate your porridge
SISSY	She had ligature marks on her wrists and her ankles consistent with being held from something like a Meat Hook for several hours
PIG	Were you inspired by that scene in Anally Ripped Whores is that one of your favourites it certainly looks like one of your favourites given that you have watched it every day for the past two years
PIG/SISSY	Are you finding this harder to hear, is this more difficult on your stomachs because we are women
SISSY	Her torso was found three metres away from her legs
PIG	Why did you do that, was it to stop her from running away
SISSY	What did you do with the portions of flesh you removed
PIG	Do you rub them on your cock when you're in your milk float?
SISSY	You tucked her intestines underneath her buttocks

PIG   Where are her shoes – her parents will want to know where her shoes are so that they can put them with her other shoes

SISSY   Why did you cut her legs up

PIG   Were you splitting her in two? Were you making it look like your cock train had driven straight through her

SISSY   You cut her mouth out, were you inspired by Deep Throat Gangbang 11

PIG   Why did you drain her stupid fucked-up goodfornothing whore blood? Did you like the look of her skin with no blood? Where on earth did you learn how to do that Do they teach you that at Milk School or is that just how they look in Skinny Fucked Up Bitches Five viewed by you on the Wednesday morning – were you checking you'd done it right – are you finding this sexy?

                People always find this sexy.

                .

SISSY   You put one of her legs on a vegetable patch underneath an Apple Tree. They're growing lettuces and violets on that patch. They've promised to name a new variety of apple after her. Laura. That's nice, isn't it.

                It could not matter less if you don't tell us where you were last Tuesday because This tells us that you were killing Laura Lahowderfisk.

                The MAN smiles.

                Perhaps PIG's drinking starts to go wrong.

Perhaps SISSY's smoking starts to go wrong. Perhaps shoes come off. Perhaps lipstick smears. Perhaps shit is on the wall.

SISSY smiles.

PIG smiles.

MAN   No it doesn't.

.

> PIG throws a full glass of whiskey down her top.
>
> SISSY leaps up from her chair.

That proves I like watching porn.

No. Not even that – that proves that I watch a lot of porn. Or. That someone with access to my computer watches a lot of porn. Nothing else

PIG   No

MAN   All that proves is that my computer wasn't being accessed at the same time as some

Psycho

was killing – Laura – did you say her name was? – but it doesn't prove much else.

.

A dental student? She didn't look like a dental student. In the photograph you just showed me.
But then. She didn't have much of a face left. So it's hard to comment.

SISSY   No

MAN   No

What?

19

.

SISSY	No
	I would. I would categorise you as an incredibly prolific Internet User
MAN	Most people are.
	I like the Internet
	You got me
PIG	The acts that were performed on Laura Lahowderfisk
MAN	That's a fucking ridiculous name
PIG	were were Identical to the ones that feature in the films you watched – Obsessively – in the weeks leading up to her murder
SISSY	I
MAN	This isn't the face of a killer
PIG	Was it not enough? The watching women get stretched by cock for ten hours a day was that not enough for you, did you stop cumming, did it start to feel mundane, did the noise *(She pulls on her cheek.)* stop being such a Big Fat Treat
MAN	Okay. Okay. I'll confess.

.

	I really like porn. I really love watching porn. I've probably got an addiction. I might try to cut it down.
SISSY	That's not
MAN	I also like consensual sex with women. I also respect my Mother. And my sister. And I like that I can have these fantasies and that they don't impact on any other aspect of my frankly blissful existence
SISSY	No that's not a a a a

MAN   Everyone watches porn

> PIG's hand slips off the table. She falls and recovers immediately.

PIG   We know

MAN   Millions of people watch this porn

> SISSY's ankle buckles. She recovers immediately.

PIG   We know

> PIG assumes a composed and powerful position.

MAN   Millions of people are watching this porn right fucking now and then eating toast and stroking their partner's face and having a conversation about the bins

PIG   We know

> SISSY's legs starts to shake.

> PIG begins to slide off the table gradually throughout.

MAN   Millions of people watch violent porn where the sole objective is to humiliate and or abuse women every single day and then they do a fun run for cancer research and give up their seat on a bus for an old man and cry at *Tristan and Isolde* or *Forrest Gump* and kiss their children and make love to their wives or their husbands holding hands and looking into the eyes of that person, their person with absolute tenderness

PIG   We know   SISSY   We know

> PIG falls off the table, slides slowly to the floor.

> SISSY grips onto the table for support as her legs give way. Her body stretches out as she slowly lowers to the floor.

21

> BEAUTIFUL MAN retrieves a suit from the
> filing cabinet and changes into it during
> the following.

MAN   I watch that every day and I turn it off and I cook my dinner and I swim in my local pool and I can look at the women in their swimming costumes there and not think anything other than oh there is a woman in a swimming costume and I hold the face of whoever I'm having sex with and kiss freckles and moles and patches of skin that are lighter or softer and sometimes I fuck them hard and sometimes we have something that is slower and what the world has told you is deeper though that would be to simplify and there's a whole range of sex we can have in between because we are complicated human beings and none of it has anything to do with the porn that I watch

and. And. And

The fact that a psycho has committed acts on your Laura Lahowderfisk that happen to also appear in porn films just proves something wonderfully comforting. That we are all connected somehow – that we are all the Same somehow, because if you've had the thought likelihood is that someone somewhere has had that thought too and made it into something that can make some fucking money.

I find that quite comforting.

.

> PIG and SISSY land on the floor in
> crumpled sitting positions.

SISSY   I. You. It's. The. For the. I.

PIG   You killed her. You watched a shitload of porn. And you killed her.

.

MAN   Prove it.

PIG	I

_____

PIG stands.

MAN	Prove it.
SISSY	I

_____

SISSY stands.

MAN	Prove it.
	.

_____

A sound. It is like an extended breath.
PIG's body contracts from the stomach.
SISSY's torso is propelled backwards.

_____

A swarming sound enters the space.

_____

BEAUTIFUL MAN puts sunglasses on.
He gets a tin of Sex from the filing cabinet.
He stands on a chair and displays the tin
to the audience.

_____

The rest of the company enter dressed
in suits and sunglasses. They appear like
sales people, each holding a tin of Sex
and displaying it to the audience.

_____

PIG and SISSY stand and face each other.

_____

Music changes to an uptempo beat

_____

PIG and SISSY move together. Regrouping,
readying to begin again. We refer to this
as 'PIG and SISSY's handshake'.

_____

SISSY puts her hand on PIG's shoulder.
PIG sweeps her arm round and they both
swing arms towards the back of the stage,
together. SISSY puts her hand on PIG's
heart. PIG puts her hand on SISSY's heart.
SISSY steps back and PIG follows, PIG
steps back and SISSY follows (like the
beginning of a cha-cha). SISSY puts her
hand on PIG's head and turns her all the
way around.

_____

They join hands and step together.
Too close.

_____

They shake hands.

2.

A throne, a red carpet and a buffet table filled with food. There is a dead swan in the middle of the carpet. Maybe SISSY throws glitter on it. The QUEEN is here. SISSY cannot contain her excitement.

PIG	Did you want us to start again? SISSY TA DA!
QUEEN	.
PIG	Sort of looking at us with this vague look on your [face]
	.
	Do you want a party ring? SISSY TA DA!
	.
	Okay. Okay. Okay.
	Okay.
	Okay I'll. Give it one last [go].
	Do you want a party ring?
	.
	Is she deaf – you failed to mention that she was / fucking deaf
SISSY	/ She's not deaf she's absolutely not deaf
PIG	Are you sure
SISSY	Hundred percent.
PIG	Are you sure she's the right one
SISSY	Uh. Yes. Obviously. Yes.
PIG	Okay well then why's she not
	.
	Party Ring. Do You Want a Fucking Party / Ring
SISSY	/ Uhhhhhh No

25

PIG	I'm Asking if she wants a party ring
SISSY	Nicely
PIG	I Am asking nicely we are happy to provide you with anything from the buffet table that you might want. Bouffet. Buffett. Ttt. buffet – am I going [mad] – buffet. right? I'm sorry I think she's cracked, this was not a good – look Lady
SISSY	UHHH *(To the QUEEN.)* / I'msosorry
PIG	/ Can you keep your shit together
SISSY	You are Shouting At Her And she is very tiny and delicate
PIG	This is weird I am finding you Weird today you're never [like this] and – Okay – Focus *(To the QUEEN.)* do you WANT anything from the Buffet table?
QUEEN	I'm sorry – I'm. I'm really terribly sorry. It's just that I. I don't know what you Mean.
PIG	Are you taking the / piss?
SISSY	/ Ahhhh
PIG	It's
SISSY	No
PIG	*(To SISSY.)* am I saying it funny?
SISSY	[I have no idea]
PIG	The table that contains the snacks and the beverages. There are very very very tiny crustless sandwiches and rainbow-coloured ice creams available. There is also homemade orangeade. It is Organic. Which you might want. To sample.
QUEEN	I'm not trying to be

	Difficult
PIG	Yes you are
QUEEN	I'm not – I'm
PIG	Could you finish your sentences faster please
SISSY	STOPIT
QUEEN	I can see that that is a buffet table and I can report that you are saying it correctly and. I appreciate the trouble you've gone to but
PIG	COULD YOU JUST FUCKING / SIGN IT PLEASE
SISSY	/ Uhhhhhhh No
PIG	I said please
QUEEN	I don't know what you want me
SISSY	No
PIG	SHE BAKED YOU A FUCKING SWAN
SISSY	STOPIT Hi.
QUEEN	The thing is is that I
SISSY	This is. It's an honour. It really is. Isn't it?
PIG	Oh, it's a dream
SISSY	Come true – it really is I can hardly believe it, can you?
PIG	. QUEEN If you would just let me No. No. And. And othernicethingsyoumightbeusedtohearing. Etcetera. Are you just going to stare at her
SISSY	Shut up. Quiet time now. For you. *(To the QUEEN.)* I like your skin it is almost translucent.

QUEEN   .

                Thank you – look, can I

SISSY   You are welcome

QUEEN   I

SISSY   Yes

QUEEN   I

SISSY   Yes Your Highest Highness

QUEEN   I don't understand what / you want

PIG   / I am going to cut her fucking / face off in a

SISSY   / NO

PIG   We got all this stuff for you lady

QUEEN   No, what You want

PIG   If I'd known you were going to be so much

QUEEN   Could you just

PIG   Fucking trouble I swear to God

QUEEN   Could I Just say   SISSY   STOP TALKING
                something   TO HER LIKE
                please can I just   THAT

PIG   I could have just Ended you

QUEEN   COULD I JUST SAY SOMETHING PLEASE.

                .

                You haven't Actually explained what you Want from
                me. Why I'm here. Why you've tied me up and
                shouted at me about buffets I don't know what you
                want you haven't said what you want and if I can give it

to you so that I can go home I will so what do you want what do you want what do you Want.

PIG   Oh.

.

It's literally just a signature

SISSY   So sorry to even ask

PIG   On a scroll – we've – we've written the Whole thing out

SISSY   Properly – with with calligraphy like you're used to

PIG   You can see we're serious

SISSY   it's a – you don't need to do Anything else

PIG   You can tell we've done this kind of shit before

SISSY   It's really very straightforward

PIG   We've waded in the law-making pool before

SISSY   It's really simple – it's Beneath you, really

PIG   We've swam those waters it's not a

SISSY   Really

PIG   big deal – it's

SISSY   We just need you to sign that.

.

QUEEN   Yes. But.
I don't know what it Is that I'm signing

PIG   THE DECREE

SISSY   Pig

QUEEN   THE CONTENT OF THE [FUCKING] DECREE.
Please.

SISSY   Porn.

               Sorry.

               We just. We want you to ban Porn.

QUEEN   Pawn?

PIG   Porn.

QUEEN   Pawn

               You want me to ban Pawn

PIG   Pornography

QUEEN   I

SISSY   We want it outlawed

PIG   Blown up

SISSY   We want it obliterated

PIG   Removed from the face of the earth

SISSY   We want it to not exist

PIG   So that we can begin again

SISSY   Yes – so that we can begin again – it's not entirely
               apocalyptic

PIG   We want you to fucking sign.
               Please.

QUEEN   Understood. But What IS it

PIG   Jesus Christ you are a piece of fucking work – it's a
               Decree, it's a scroll, it's a Law we got you cocktail
               sausages don't you Do this all the fucking time I'm
               Tired and I'm Furious but I'm also confused and I am
               so so Sad too because because there's no Depiction
               here, okay – just to be clear / there's no no no Gap
               here

SISSY   / there's no no no Gap here

PIG	There's no safe bit where it all exists as a Concept or Idea or or Fantasy okay, just because it's named as that, just because there has been such an enormous lack of specificity with That Word – FANTASY – does not mean it can be Hijacked and own that meaning – what you end up Watching Is – by its very nature, what ends up on screen is an act or series of acts that Has Actually Happened To Those People and that cannot be disregarded – it is a tangible event and it happened all so that you can jerk off and I find that it's a Law we want you to pass and we know you can we checked really thoroughly so could you just do it please
QUEEN	Pornography. What is Pornography
PIG	.
	You do know that your ankles are bleeding, don't you? Your skin is fucking paper, if we need to make that tie any tighter we absolutely will
QUEEN	I don't know what Porn
SISSY	Ography
QUEEN	Is – I don't know what you want me to ban and I won't ban something I don't Know – that's ludicrous
SISSY	That is ludicrous.
PIG	Sex
SISSY	Not sex
QUEEN	Pornography is sex – you want me to ban sex
PIG	NO SISSY No
QUEEN	I don't want to ban Sex I don't think I should ban sex
PIG	No no no no no – neither do I – neither do we – I. Not Sex. It's Not sex. That's the [point] – that's the Whole [point] – it's Not Sex it's

31

SISSY	It's the printed or visual material containing the explicit description or display of sexual organs or activity, intended to stimulate sexual excitement
PIG	Except that that's not it
SISSY	Except that that doesn't Explain it at all
QUEEN	It's Watching other people have sex?
SISSY	No PIG No
SISSY	But sort of
PIG	Essentially – [Yes] but that's not It, that doesn't explain
QUEEN	Okay – it's Looking at genitalia
PIG	No SISSY No
SISSY	But it Can be
PIG	But that doesn't Summarise the the [experience] of it – it's not it even a little bit – it's um. It's. You can't – if you haven't Seen it it doesn't make much, it's. It's not. I don't know how to – are you Sure you don't know what it is – It's
SISSY	It's
QUEEN	It's
PIG	It's
	It's hard to [explain]
	Okay, so. No. Okay. No. So what it Feels like – what it Feels like to watch is. What it Feels like
	is um

___

PIG beckons SISSY over.

___

It is important that PIG is always 'doing' to SISSY's body. The movement is forced on SISSY, but she is always willing and compliant. The movement should look violent but the tone between the two performers is friendly. They check in with each other at various stages to see how they are both doing.

Sequence:

PIG pushes SISSY backwards and forwards with her hands. Warming up.

PIG grabs SISSY around the arms and upper body and swings her from side to side in a wide circle. It repeats.

PIG pushes SISSY's head down and SISSY collapses then stands up immediately. It repeats.

PIG pushes SISSY forwards, SISSY falls to her knees

PIG sits behind SISSY and roughly grabs handfuls of her body – mainly breasts and face – repeatedly.

PIG grabs SISSY's wrists and holds them behind her body, she flings her forwards and backwards. SISSY's head jerks. It repeats.

PIG grabs SISSY's hair and throws her onto her side.

PIG kneels on SISSY's ribs and waist and bounces on her aggressively, repeatedly.

PIG grabs SISSY's hair and pushes her forwards onto her hands and knees.

PIG forces SISSY's body to the ground but SISSY comes back up. It repeats.

PIG kicks SISSY to one side.

PIG throws SISSY's legs. Her body is flung and rolled around the space. It repeats.

SISSY lies on her back, PIG offers her a hand up but just as she is about to reach balance, PIG lets go, and she falls to the floor. It repeats.

PIG leaves.

They both recover immediately.

And then it's um – yeah no. Like. So you feel
Like that

SISSY	I suppose
PIG	If that makes any
SISSY	Yeah, if that's At all.
QUEEN	.
SISSY	Are you alright?
QUEEN	Feel a bit sick.
PIG	Yeah
SISSY	Do you need a bucket?
QUEEN	Could you untie me
SISSY	Or a fondant fancy or or
QUEEN	Perhaps you could untie me
SISSY	Eclair or something or
QUEEN	Or you could untie me
PIG	Will you sign?
QUEEN	I don't understand
PIG	Okay, Look Lady
QUEEN	No
PIG	This is going on fucking everywhere okay and you Don't Get It I
QUEEN	I DO GET IT SHUT UP I GET IT.

I understand what you've just shown me – I GET it. It's just. Aren't people having sex?

SISSY	. PIG .
QUEEN	Don't people want to have sex anymore?
SISSY	Yes
PIG	All the evidence would point to
SISSY	I mean, clearly, yes
PIG	That's not what we're
SISSY	This is not About sex
QUEEN	Well, no. Clearly. That wasn't sex, what you just did – that's not what sex feels like.
PIG	No.
QUEEN	Not what sex feels like At All
PIG	No
SISSY	Right. No. Sure. I mean. I don't. I wouldn't. But. Okay.
QUEEN	Do people Think this is sex? This. Porn
SISSY	Ography
QUEEN	Do they think that that's sex?
SISSY	It Is. Technically.
QUEEN	No
PIG	No Sissy
QUEEN	It's not
PIG	Though, Biologically speaking
QUEEN	No
SISSY	Well. I mean. It is.

QUEEN	No. What you just did. That's not how sex feels
PIG	Sure. Okay.
	.
	Say more things
QUEEN	Biologically, you might be able to say that your porn / is sex
SISSY	/ Not Ours – just to clarify
PIG	Mmmhmm, go on
QUEEN	That Technically the two are the same
SISSY	we were just demonstrating, we don't Partake or or or
QUEEN	But Sex.
	What sex Is – what it makes you Feel – what the Sensation is is
SISSY	Is
PIG	Shuttup Is
QUEEN	Is. It's hard to [explain] but it's. It's.

> This sequence was made in response to exploring a variety of different sensations, experiences and tastes. For example, embodying the sharp, zingy taste of a lemon, or exploring the experience of being a body in complete darkness, trying to discover what's around you. It should not simulate or mimic the shapes or acts of sex. It is about sensation.

> The work was always entirely physical, not verbal, but vocalising is always welcome.

> We workshopped this several times. We always improvised with our eyes closed.

> We worked sometimes with imagination, e.g.

> be in complete darkness

you are surrounded by very hot water

you are being tickled by three feathers
simultaneously - we want to see where
they are and how you feel about the
sensation of each one

you are surrounded by hot golden syrup,
up to your neck

you're an old cat

an electric shock

We worked by embodying flavours,
feeding the actors food and letting them
improvise, e.g.

a lemon

a gherkin

dark chocolate

peanut butter

a date

a raspberry

Wotsits

We then refined and choreographed the
most interesting and articulate movements
and placed them in a sequence that is
varied and rich in tempo and texture.

Sometimes in between thoughts THE
QUEEN can say 'It feels like' and 'It's like'
to help the performer reach from one
contrasting sensation to another.

As the movement begins, PIG unties THE
QUEEN's ankles.

Below are a few examples of movement in
the sequence.

THE QUEEN is in the dark. She explores
the space around her.

She is on her throne. She has her eyes closed and reaches with her right hand out to one side. Her weight tips over and she swings her legs onto the arm of the throne and stretches out, like a cat. She slides so that she is upside down and uncurls her limbs gradually until she is fully extended.

THE QUEEN embodies the taste of dark chocolate.

She is on her knees. She opens her chest and head, up and back as she takes a sharp breath in. She is propelled forwards, but catches herself with her hands, and yields gently into the floor. Her eyes widen as she falls. She is surprised and delighted.

THE QUEEN embodies the taste of raspberries.

She gallops around the space like she's at a ceilidh, she swings her arms, the movement is released. She covers the entire space.

At the end of the sequence THE QUEEN takes in the audience, then settles back into her throne.

In our sequence there are nineteen little pieces of choreography. It lasts about five minutes.

SISSY   Oh.

PIG   OH.

QUEEN   Are you okay?

PIG   Feel a bit funny

QUEEN   Yes

SISSY   It's. It's Interesting

PIG   Bit

	Ummmm
	Funny
QUEEN	I'm sure
SISSY	Not my sort of
PIG	In a Good way
QUEEN	Yes
SISSY	thing but. Yeah. Fair enough and
PIG	In a really Really good way
QUEEN	Yes
SISSY	looks nice and – so yes could we move to the
PIG	In a really sort of
SISSY	decree again – back to the issue of
PIG	YEAH sort of want to
QUEEN	Yes
SISSY	Signing and
PIG	get INVOLVED or or or
QUEEN	Yes
SISSY	But first First maybe we could get to the the point of
PIG	have a fucking PARTY or
QUEEN	Absolutely
SISSY	We could first of all
PIG	A Party with my BODY d'you know what I what I mean
QUEEN	I do
SISSY	BUT FIRST we could maybe get you to Sign the decree

A bit.

Just here.

If you wouldn't mind?

QUEEN .

I've never done anything like that before.

SISSY No. Sure, well. That's fine, you can start now just here dotted line

QUEEN I've never just passed a law on my own

SISSY Right, but. You can do Now which is great for you – I think you will feel really Empowered if you just sign it

QUEEN I Should sign it

SISSY You should sign it, yes PIG You should sign it, yes

QUEEN I think I Will sign it

SISSY Brilliant PIG Excellent choice

QUEEN I'm going to bloody sign it

SISSY That's wonderful PIG That's a strong move

QUEEN Yes

SISSY Yes

PIG Yes

She signs the decree.

There is a big party. It's brilliant.

The party is tightly choreographed. It is in the style of a music video to a current pop track with an upbeat tempo.

It is a combination of choreography in unison, and the creation of big images of celebration. Props from the scene such as a champagne bottle and glasses, and three huge union jack flags are used. It all feels like a cartoon of patriotism, it is very

British. THE QUEEN parties just as hard as PIG and SISSY. They make fun references to our actual Queen such as riding the union jack flags like horses.

Our version of 'The Macarena' appears for the first time in this number.

It is a simple sequence made up of six counts of eight and can be performed solo or in a group. It has a '90s party' vibe, and includes moves from music videos like 'Tragedy' and '5,6,7,8' by Steps, and the funky chicken.

The music cuts out at a surprising point – just as they are reaching the climax of the action.

They look up. It suddenly feels cold. The party deflates.

QUEEN   I'm sorry.

PIG   It didn't [work].

SISSY   Oh.

PIG   I'm cold

SISSY   My lungs hurt

PIG   Again

SISSY   If I cough them out they'll be black and dried out and like dust

PIG   I can taste blood in my mouth

QUEEN   I've never tried before – I've never Known if I had the

          Capacity to

          EnForce that sort of

The company invade the space. They are uptempo and cheery. They are dressed in delivery uniforms with hats and sunglasses. They are each carrying a pack

41

of Sex tins. They deliver the tins to an
audience member and begin the scene
change.

Anything or.

SISSY   No

PIG   Right, sure

SISSY   Of course I'm worried about the next generation of
               course I am – that's a huge part of it but I'm also a
               lot worried about me – is it alright to want something
               better for ourselves is it alright to want to begin again
               because I'm worried about the sex I am signing up for
               because of porn and

QUEEN   And you seemed so very certain

SISSY   Yes

PIG   We always are

QUEEN   That I thought it might

PIG   No.

SISSY   No.

QUEEN   .

               I feel so very sad my heart might crack.

3.

'PIG and SISSY's handshake'.

A classroom, full of empty chairs. The LITTLE BOY sits on a chair.
He swings his legs.

A pause. About ten seconds. And then some.

This is full pelt. As fast as you can. Seven minutes is too long.

PIG	Do you need us to start that bit again did you hear it all it's just the bit about if you sit there for a bit and we'll explain and it will be sort of [okay] except I don't know that it will do you need a cushion or
SISSY	No
PIG	I
SISSY	No
PIG	It's
SISSY	No
PIG	Because he's
SISSY	No
PIG	small and
SISSY	No
PIG	I'm finding this
SISSY	STOP
PIG	I
SISSY	Here you are here you are here you are a little thing a little curve of a thing a little turn of the moon red red raw brand brilliant new not so long here a little being making a mark on the world just beginning to make an imprint on the world your face your hair your eyes are all still so Incredibly New does your mother still rock

                you to sleep some nights that is bringing it into sharp
                focus how very small you are

PIG   My lungs

SISSY   No

PIG   There's blood

SISSY   I

PIG   My feet are turning black I

SISSY   NOT FAIR   PIG   NOT FAIR

SISSY   there is nothing wrong with watching other people
                have sex or enjoying viewing another naked body – it
                has the very great potential to be a beautiful wonderful
                thing – but that is Not what we have that is Not the
                thing that we have gifted ourselves

PIG   And the ethical stuff, the feminist stuff the stuff that's
                out there that Doesn't degrade women isn't worth this
                tsunami of stuff that does – I will not be Distracted by
                that because it is the shittest consolation prize on the
                planet NO

SISSY   NO

PIG   NO a beginning you are just beginning you are a whole
                armful of brand news and potentials and once upon a's
                but the world hasn't been gotten ready yet the world
                wasn't prepared the whole world didn't make itself
                good enough for your arrival and I am sorry because
                you are on the cusp of something you are on the very
                edge of it now you are making your way to school now
                year one / is your coat peg a fish and your rucksack a
                frog you must like under the sea things

SISSY   / is your coat peg a fish and your rucksack a frog you
                must like under the sea things very much your star
                badge is full of gold stars well done you and you go to
                school with your Mum and your sister you stop at the

park for seven goes on the slide like a superhero and she kisses you round the corner from the school gate so that nobody sees this but so that you still get a kiss and you get a gold star in Arithmetic and a gold star in story time and another star in gymnastics when you fly over the horse like a Real Life Superhero hard hard it's in my throat like a stopping a stopping my breath / and and and

PIG   / and and and one day one day soon perhaps tomorrow or the next day or the day after that one day after gymnastics at break a boy a boy in your class perhaps or a boy in a class one bigger than your class will say he has something to show you will say he has something to show you and you'll swap him three Wotsits and he will take a phone out of his grey shorts pocket and he will show you a six second a six second can't hold it too heavy a six second

SISSY   a six second video of a woman with no clothes on sucking on a willy like it's a lollipop and he'll say it is called sex and you'll drop your crisps and you'll laugh even though you think you would like to cry pick it up now my heart's exploded all over my ribcage and is spilling out

PIG   and you will feel sick and like you would like to lie down for a little bit and that you can't ever not see what you just saw which of course you can't and it will begin it will start there because it's not your fault it's not your fault it is so entirely not your fault the fault belongs to the world because we were supposed to make it better before little boys as glorious as you came along before we had the Audacity to bring new life along we should have looked down and realised we are neck deep in a world that is not worthy and begin again it will begin

SISSY   begin and you'll wait at the school gates and want to bury your face in your mother's stomach and have it so it never happened and you'll get home and later you'll type Sex into Google and you'll click and you'll cry and you'll watch and you'll click and you'll watch and when your Dad brings you up a glass of lemonade you'll want to hide deep in his stomach but can't can't can't

PIG   And you'll click and you'll watch and you'll click and you'll watch and this will repeat and you'll go into school the next day and show the other boys and some of them will show you And you'll click and you'll watch and you'll type Lollipop Willies into Google and Sex Sex Sex Sex Sex and NO CAN'T
WON'T

SISSY   into Google and you'll watch Big Tits Big Whores and And on you'll go you'll watch Three Holes Nine Cocks and and in the school playground and your none of this is / and you'll get a girlfriend at Big School and you'll watch and watch and watch

PIG   / and you'll get a girlfriend at Big School and you'll watch and watch and watch and you'll make her do things before you tell her you like her and you'll call her a whore you don't know that word do you but you'll call her a

SISSY   and you'll watch and you'll not be able to have sex with a girl without calling her a whore and and

PIG   you'll grow up and one day you'll meet a nice girl a girl who a girl who a

SISSY   a girl who makes your heart light and she is the the the

PIG   funniest person you'll ever meet Hands Down and this is because we need to make the world better and you'll go travelling together and you'll have baths together and eat together and she will be really good at getting you to talk about your feelings and she is all the way the kindest person you have ever met her capacity for kindness consistently overwhelms you but but

SISSY/PIG   It won't have changed it won't have stopped

SISSY	you'll hold her face when you fuck her you'll hold her head and you'll watch the screen and you'll call her a whore and she'll gag and you'll promise to stop it you'll promise to sort your shit out when her stomach starts filling with the bones of another and you'll promise to talk to someone as you put your ear at her full full belly kicking with a baby a baby a

Tiny pause.

PIG	This is because the world can't get better with you in it.
SISSY	I can't.
PIG	I know.
	Show me where you are breaking.
SISSY	All over.
PIG	And when the baby girl arrives and someone puts it in your arms you'll look at it and imagine how it could all be about to begin again with the whole world readying to hurt your little girl like you did and you'll put your ear up to your baby girl's stomach and you'll listen and you'll bury your hair in all that softness and you'll weep and we didn't make the world good enough

SISSY shoots him.

She drops the gun.

SISSY	Next one.
	Get the next one.
	Get the next fucking one.
PIG	I'm cold.
	My hair's falling out.
	My bones are breaking.
	It's not working. It didn't [work]. It's not [working].

PIG and SISSY come towards the LITTLE BOY. They sit him up. They all look at the audience for a beat.

Leads into...

A trio. A thank you. An hello. An 'of course we haven't killed him, really. He's our friend'.

PIG offers her hand to LITTLE BOY who stands up willingly. PIG pushes him gently backwards and he falls into SISSY's arms and they all walk back together for three steps.

PIG turns to walk away but leaves her hand behind her. LITTLE BOY takes her hand and walks with her. She lifts her arms and he turns under it so he is facing her.

PIG steps back as LITTLE BOY puts his arm around SISSY's shoulders, and SISSY spins LITTLE BOY around on her hip. LITTLE BOY lands and walks off. Exits.

As LITTLE BOY leaves, PIG and SISSY see that they have blood on their hands. They look at their hands.

The following is a duet between PIG and SISSY. They take it in turns to take each other's weight, and give their own weight to the other. This is a regroup. This is performed like a conversation. Their first language is movement. No angst. Or as little as possible, given what has just happened.

They are both examining their upturned hands. SISSY walks towards PIG. She goes to put her hands on PIG's, but PIG moves them at the last minute, hooks her arms under SISSY's arms, lifts her, and steps backwards with her. Puts her down.

SISSY lifts PIG so PIG sits on her waist with her legs wrapped around her. They turn. SISSY puts PIG down.

PIG turns so they are facing the same way. SISSY is draped around her shoulders. PIG drags her across the space. Diagonal journey.

They stand. SISSY turns so they are back to back. They nuzzle each other with the back of their heads.

SISSY lowers to the floor. PIG follows. SISSY crawls. PIG is draped across her back, open limbs, staring at the ceiling.

PIG slides off and sweeps her leg around so she is sitting with her legs on either side of SISSY's body.

They roll sideways together. PIG over SISSY, until they are siting next to each other. They look at each other. PIG's arm is loosely around SISSY's shoulders.

They roll backwards together. They are sitting on their knees.

They roll sideways together and sweep round and up. They are standing next to each other. They look at each other.

They lean into a run. PIG takes SISSY's arms and lowers her into a tango lean.

SISSY comes up and PIG leans sideways into SISSY. Hip to hip. They come up.

PIG tucks her hips under SISSY and swings her round in a circle.

They stand facing each other. PIG pushes SISSY's forehead lightly, so she falls back. PIG catches her, and they take a few steps together. They come up to standing. SISSY holds PIG's lower back as PIG tips backwards, opening her chest and neck to the sky. They come up.

PIG falls back into SISSY and they turn together.

PIG drapes over SISSY's shoulders. They walk together, around the edge of the stage.

They reach the centre.

'PIG and SISSY's handshake.'

They shake hands.

4.

The Internet. There might be vending machines and there might be some tins of Sex, just visible hanging around. A girl, around 12 years old – THE MEGA HACKER – is here.

> PIG and SISSY complete all of the movement and actions instructed by MEGA HACKER in this.

HACKER   I'm gonna need you bitches to start again okay.

Cos.

You just came in here and said a whole bunch of shit at me in hysterical high-pitched voices and I'm kind of pissed off.

PIG   We're very sorry

HACKER   Uh huh

SISSY   We're so sorry

HACKER   Shut up now I mean you can start again

SISSY   That would be Really

HACKER   You need to shut up faster – but like, only if I feel like it but I'm not totally unreasonable, like I'm really really reasonable mostly, so, it's, like worth your asking if you can tell me why the fuck you're here and stuff

.

Whyisn'tanyonesayinganythingI'mreallyborednow

SISSY   We would be

HACKER   Not you. You. Piggy. You say something

PIG   We'd be really grateful

HACKER   Yeah

PIG   And can show our gratitude

HACKER   Uh huh yeah

PIG	If you. If you would consider turning the Internet off
HACKER	Yeah
PIG	The whole thing – if you would shut the entire Internet down so that it can never be switched back on for anybody ever then
HACKER	Yeah
PIG	Then we would really be indebted to you forevermore and
HACKER	Yeah
PIG	Yeah
HACKER	Sure – do a dance for me – but I guess, like why I would – do a dance for me now
SISSY	A
HACKER	Shutup I don't like the tone of your voice it's grating – choreograph a dance for me and make it really good and and like we're on Broadway or

> PIG and SISSY begin dancing 'The Macarena' in the style of 'Broadway'.

	Yeah and okay, so you're like, I'm just Processing Old, I guess. And so you haven't figured out how it could be really good for you or something
PIG	No – no, that's not
HACKER	*(To SISSY)* You can talk now, just don't use your actual voice, make it
SISSY	Okay
HACKER	Yeah, like deeper and stuff and
SISSY	I
HACKER	Yeah that's good

SISSY	We understand the
HACKER	I'm impressed
SISSY	Thank you
HACKER	With your voice that's good, you've impressed me, keep dancing bitches and make it sexy, make it like your bodies are much better than they actually are and yeah

PIG and SISSY begin to dance more 'sexy'.

PIG	the the imagining a new space, a new beginning – that is HARD because it – Porn – is really about capitalism, yes, okay, stay with me, which is huge because ideally we want to dismantle that and say let's try and not Monetise this / THANK YOU ALL SO MUCH FOR PAYING TO SEE THIS BY THE WAY
SISSY	/ THANK YOU ALL SO MUCH FOR PAYING TO SEE THIS BY THE WAY
PIG	We understand the benefits of the Internet
HACKER	Yeah
PIG	It's a really useful tool
HACKER	Yeah
SISSY	It's impossible to imagine life without it sometimes
PIG	But there Was life without it
HACKER	That's true – faster now, do it all much more like you're in a good music video by someone really fucked up and cool that you would never have heard of much much much faster than that

PIG and SISSY try to dance faster and more 'cool'.

PIG	And it was okay and although, you know, we'd miss it
SISSY	Very much

PIG   It's really about the bigger picture at this point

HACKER   You're fucking cracked, dance like you're on MDMA now

PIG   I'm sorry, how d'you mean, cracked

HACKER   You're shy about some of the sexy pictures and now you want to take the Whole Fucking Internet away that equals CRACKED lady

PIG   I'm not shy

SISSY   She's not shy

PIG   I'm not shy about sexy stuff, I'm really Into sexy stuff, that's not the

HACKER   AND NOW LET'S ACTUALLY TAKE MDMA KEEP DANCING BITCHES

PIG   okay – but, so that's not the point, a lot of what's out there isn't really sexy

HACKER   You don't Own the definition of sexy

PIG   Yes, fair, but .

HACKER   That's what this is about right, you want to control what people get to fuck to or eat to or hug to or kiss to or suck toes to or whatever else they want to get up to in an entirely legal fashion – YOU don't like it and you think that gives you the right to take it away from everyone else

SISSY   No, no, that's not what, that's not it's it's

HACKER   Stop stuttering it's giving me a brain tumour which I will cut out and make you eat and watch you shit it out and feed it to Miss Piggy dance like you're fat bitches with fat asses. Fatter than that. Fatter. Much much fatter.

PIG and SISSY continue 'The Macarena' like they have very fat bodies.

	Yeah. Yeah that's the good stuff, that's the sweet spot – are you religious nutjobs
PIG	No – no, that's a common misconception but – and really doesn't come into / the picture
HACKER	Are you the Pope
SISSY	As in
HACKER	Or Jesus
SISSY	It's actually that there's a lot of stuff that's incredibly degrading and
PIG	Are you sure you even know what's out there
HACKER	That is laughable that is offensive I am offended okay you've really fucking offended me
SISSY	You've offended her
PIG	That wasn't my intention
HACKER	Slap yourselves. Harder – keep dancing, of Course I know what's out there I've frigged off to All of it lady hell I did it to my Mum getting done by a horse dance like you hate your body much much faster than that – it's no big deal

> PIG and SISSY do 'The Macarena' but like they hate their bodies.

SISSY	See now, no judgement
PIG	the fuck are you doing
SISSY	But, I would suggest that that Is quite a big deal
HACKER	Masturbation, old ladies, Not a big deal anymore
PIG	Absolutely SISSY Couldn't agree more
HACKER	Make me fly, I don't give a shit how but I know you can do it because you are batshit cray cray

> PIG and SISSY carry HACKER around the space on their shoulders.

SISSY/PIG	THIS HAS JUST BEEN ABOUT HETEROSEXUAL PORN – THAT IS A FAILURE. THIS IS NOT AN APOLOGY
SISSY	I just wonder
HACKER	YEAH BABY sounds like your voice again
SISSY	I just wonder if you need to investigate how okay it is that you're getting off on a series of degrading and violent and and offensive images
HACKER	You're not my therapist
SISSY	That's true
HACKER	I Skype him on a Tuesday and that is my business
SISSY	Fair enough – that is fair enough but I
HACKER	Haven't you bitches ever heard of freedom of speech

PIG	Yes	SISSY	Yes

HACKER	PUT ME DOWN I'M GONNA VOMIT A SHOWER OF BISCUITS ON YOUR FACES AND NOW CLIMB HER LIKE A FUCKING TREE and haven't you

> PIG makes a wide base and attempts to look like a tree. SISSY climbs her as high as she can and then attempts to look like a tree.

bitches ever heard of freedom of thought

PIG	Yes	SISSY	Yes

HACKER	And freedom of expression

PIG	Yes	SISSY	Yes

HACKER	And also, of fucking Censorship climb her better

PIG	Yes	SISSY	Yes

HACKER	Porn is freedom

PIG   I would question that

SISSY   I would refute that very strongly

HACKER   When you're done climbing her, climb her again but better because that did not impress me and I know you psychos are capable of impressing me, who are you to

SISSY runs and jumps onto PIG's shoulders.

Police the fucking World like that, how dare you tell me what I can and can't watch when everything's between Consenting Paid Willing adults who get to fuck for MONEY do you have any idea how great that is and you're Censoring it

SISSY   You're censoring my right to exist in the world without being sexualised and degraded at every opportunity every time I want to wear something that reminds you of sex because everything is porn every time I eat a banana or a a a a

HACKER   STUTTERING again you actually eat Bananas you put those yellow Bananas in your mouth that is fucking nasty lady SLAP YOURSELVES REALLY HARD AND GET ON THE FLOOR AND DO SOME SIT-UPS show me your squishy old lady abs

SISSY   I'd also take a bit of an issue with the Consenting Paid Adults part

HACKER   Oh I bet you do, you gonna spout me some Horseyshit about the words Consent and Choice not really meaning anything in a deeply patriarchal capitalist society faster push-ups bitches, I want them fucking faster

SISSY   Well – Yes actually

HACKER   THAT IS PATRONISING, OF COURSE A WOMAN CAN CHOOSE TO FUCK FOR MONEY

SISSY THAT MAY BE
THE CASE BUT
HER CHOICE
TO DO SO
FUCKS OVER   HACKER   Oh really? really?
EVERY WOMAN   Shouting? You
WHO ISN'T   gonna keep
MAKING THAT   shouting? You think
CHOICE IN A   shouting is a clever
FREE WAY IT IS   idea
INDIVIDUALISM
AND IT SHOWS
COMPLETE
DISREGARD
FOR THE
ENTIRE HUMAN   PIG   Stop shouting
POPULATION

HACKER   Shut the fuck up

SISSY   Yes

HACKER   Make yourselves fucking dizzy you're depraved

PIG   Like

HACKER   Spin round spin round – really really fast, keep
            spinning til I tell you to stop – you do know that
            actually everyone's fine don't you

SISSY   I'm not sure I

HACKER   Like, the world's pretty different from what you grew
            up with, from what you might have been promised
            because you're old saggy bitches and we're a new breed
            and we're pretty fucking resilient okay – faster faster
            faster – and we're Okay with the world we've got, the
            world we Inherited from you fuckers – we're Well
            Equipped to deal with it all okay, you people think
            you get the world you deserve and you do and we're

building it and we're coping with it and we're okay with it and we're growing from it and learning from it and quite a lot of us don't actually give a shit about it because we're evolving and we're not actually all that damaged – SPIN FUCKING FASTER I WANNA SEE YOU VOMIT UP YOUR SPLEENS BITCHES – and you could put your energy into something a hell of a lot more worthy like war or famine or fucking ass cancer now pick her up like she's a wheelbarrow and go quick

SISSY   I'm

HACKER   You gonna be sick

SISSY   No

HACKER   Then get to it cos you disgust me

> PIG is the front and SISSY is the back of a human wheelbarrow. PIG paddles with her hands as fast as she can. It's very difficult.

SISSY   It's depressing that we have to put up with it – that humanity is evolving to Endure it

HACKER   You know you're gonna have to go a helluva lot faster than that – maybe we LIKE it and we're okay with it, maybe we LOVE it AND we're not damaged by it, that ever enter your tiny minds

PIG   Yes   SISSY   Yes

HACKER   I take that back your minds are not tiny they are big now lick the floor.

PIG   I

HACKER   Lick it clean

> PIG is licking the floor and trying to be clear at the same time

PIG   I'm not sure that Is okay, you must have to dehumanise an awful lot of women to be okay with it and to love it

and I don't think dehumanising anyone is actually okay
and also maybe I have some faith in a better world

HACKER   Literally didn't get a single word of that cos your
           tongue was on the floor and that's nasty now I'm gonna
           need some press-ups from you now – drop and give me
           twenty and if they're shitty I'll just make you start over
           – like that one, start over

PIG   I know it's
           extreme – we
           do know it's
           extreme – we do
           Appreciate that,   HACKER   Start again.
           I am not so far
           removed from
           the world that I   .
           cannot process
           And again. that   And again.
           asking you to
           switch off the   .
           Internet so that
           we can End   Start again.
           All porn is an
           extreme thing but   .
           it has got to the
           stage where we   .
           need something
           radical and we   Start again.
           need to begin
           again and we   .
           need to begin to
           imagine entirely   .
           new landscapes
           which is difficult,   Start again.
           which is a huge
           ask, we know that

HACKER	I'm gonna get on your back and take a nap whilst you do your press-ups Piggy cos you're finding this too easy

> MEGA HACKER balances on PIG's legs and she moves her up and down.

	– you, keep going and you you give me fifty eye blinks on the double
SISSY	Eye blinks
HACKER	Don't talk back lady, fifty of 'em
PIG	But a Bold one and a Big one and the one we should be asking for – we're not reaching for apocalyptic here – we're not saying Switch Off the Internet, End all Porn and Nothing that's not what we're saying
HACKER	You're doing a shitty job of saying otherwise, naptime now

> PIG lets HACKER down.

> SISSY turns HACKER into a romantic tango lean.

SISSY	We want to begin again

> HACKER comes up and walks away.

HACKER	DANCE AGAIN BITCHES

> HACKER turns back.

	hang on now, you want to what?
SISSY / PIG	We want to begin again.
SISSY	We want to end it all. And begin again
HACKER	You're nuts old lady this is the world, you get the world you deserve you get the society you deserve we made this now fucking wallow in it dance faster dance like you're in a fucking porno

61

> The Music gets louder. PIG and SISSY grab at each other's bodies. They cover the whole stage, climbing all over the set, rubbing their bodies against the floor, the HACKER, each other. It is fast and frenetic. It screams of desperation.

SISSY   I disagree

PIG   I believe in our ability to make something better

SISSY   I believe in the human capacity to change and do something

HACKER   Well we haven't fucking done it so far.

          Holy shitbags, take a look at yourselves.

          She turns the music off.

          You're pathetic old old ladies look at you you're a fucking nightmare.

          .

          Keep dancing.

          And look at that you just keep dancing.

          Okay.

          .

          She turns the Internet off.

          It's off.

> They stop dancing.

          .

          PIG might cry.

> They all fall to the floor. PIG and SISSY gaze up.

SISSY   Tired?

PIG   No

SISSY   Feels

PIG	Better, I feel better it feels better
SISSY	I don't know what to
PIG	do, I know it's it's
SISSY	weird my eyes feel
PIG	normal, head feels lighter it's
HACKER	I'm scared
PIG	better – thank you
HACKER	Can you pick me up
SISSY	We should [go]
PIG	Air feels cleaner even it's
SISSY	my limbs feel less heavy there's a
HACKER	Can you pick me up
SISSY	can't explain it – something light around my ribcage
PIG	Better just feel, I just feel better shall we [go]
HACKER	Can you lift me up please
	.
PIG	No
SISSY	But thank you for your
HACKER	Can you carry me please
PIG	No
HACKER	Can you hold me please I'm hurting all this space around me is making me feel
SISSY	No – we need to
HACKER	Please can you lift me up and hold me I feel frightened
PIG	No, that's not

It starts to rain.

I

MEGA HACKER starts to cry.

HACKER   Please hold me

SISSY   Don't even think about it

PIG   But she's

HACKER   Please

PIG   I don't know what to I

HACKER   Please I don't want to be on my own.

MEGA HACKER climbs onto PIG's back.
_____
They all stand and look at the audience.
_____
MEGA HACKER climbs onto SISSY's hip.
_____
MEGA HACKER climbs into PIG's arms.
_____
MEGA HACKER climbs onto SISSY's back.

5.

PIG	Um. I
SISSY	We have to
PIG	Can you
SISSY	No
PIG	It's just that she's
SISSY	No
PIG	Can we just Refocus and
SISSY	Trying
PIG	Want to do something
SISSY	Okay
PIG	Good with all this this
SISSY	She's
PIG	Space and
SISSY	Heavy
PIG	Light and
SISSY	My head
PIG	It's – okay – it's – there's a Responsibility now
SISSY	Yes – Can you
PIG	Already
SISSY	She wants you
PIG	Well than can you
SISSY	Beginning again and doing something Good
PIG	Yes because we've done this this this

SISSY	This Enormous thing and
PIG	Yes
SISSY	And now there's. There's – what's the [word]
PIG	Nothing
SISSY	No
PIG	Emptiness
SISSY	No
PIG	Barren Lands
SISSY	Stop it – Opportunity
PIG	Opportunity
SISSY	To do
PIG	is that soil
SISSY	Where
PIG	On your
SISSY	Where are we
PIG	I don't know – I'm starting to to [panic] to – can you hear water or
SISSY	No – no, okay, no, we were saying, let's refocus, let's, this is important now Opportunity
PIG	Opportunity
SISSY	Opportunity to
PIG	To
SISSY	To Build something
PIG	Yes – to build something or or Make something or at least make Space for something – does that make Sense or

SISSY	Yes, very good, it's very – can we put her [down] yet or
PIG	No
SISSY	No
PIG	She's – so – she's – but let's, try to Ignore her and – let's just, put her up
SISSY	Okay – so Opportunity to Begin Again and make something new and and –
PIG	What's the opposite of it all
SISSY	I
PIG	To begin again with with kindness
SISSY	With kindness
PIG	With a new capacity for

An OLD MAN appears carrying two heavy bags of shopping.

The MEGA HACKER stops crying.

He stares.

They stare.

OLD MAN   I don't know where I live.

They stare.

He stares.

OLD MAN   I don't know where I
Come from – does everybody Come From [somewhere] or – .
I can't remember where I – .

He stares.

They stare.

He leaves.

The MEGA HACKER starts to cry again.

PIG   I

SISSY   No

PIG   Is it

SISSY   No

PIG   Happening again or

SISSY   No – make a Good thing, make a a a

PIG   Begin again begin again, we always said begin again

SISSY   What's the again

PIG   Exactly

SISSY   What's the bit that's after the now

PIG   Exactly

SISSY   What's the Next – what's the very

The OLD MAN enters.

They stare.

He stares.

The MEGA HACKER stops crying.

OLD MAN   I thought it was back by the roundabout – the roundabout with the yellow roses, but there's a duck pond there with three ducks and that makes me sure it must be this way but I don't remember and there's nothing at the bottom of my pockets but for paper. But paper

PIG   Stop it.

OLD MAN   It's my birthday today. I've had twenty-nine thousand birthdays if you count every day – there will be candles on cakes and big bears from my children.

SISSY	Stop it
OLD MAN	Four children, four babes and one that flew and three that grew tall like greenhouses, like greenhouses for sunflowers until they could fit in grown-up shoes, they'll be waiting at home for me. Time gets lost in butterfly dives and tiny bugs in their scribbly hair and happy birthdays to you can you help me find my house please, my hands are hurting and I don't know why.
PIG	We can't help you
OLD MAN	I thought it was back by the water but there are apple trees and the roundabout with pink roses makes me certain it's this way
PIG	We can't help you
OLD MAN	My hands are hurting and I don't know why
SISSY	Go away

He drops his shopping bags. He looks at them. They look at them.

OLD MAN	I can't find my house
PIG	That's not our
OLD MAN	My hands are hurting
SISSY	Please can you
OLD MAN	I can't remember if anyone is waiting for me, I can't remember if there will be candles on a cake or dancing on my feet or whether my Mother will be there in bloom, I can't find my way home. Perhaps it's back by that slide. Or near those allotments by that motorway. Is that why I can't breathe?
	I can't remember where my house is.
	Will you help me?

There is silence. Then.

CHAPTER 1. THEY PLAY.

OLD MAN starts to play physically with PIG, SISSY and MEGA HACKER.

There are a series of simple, physical, joyful, non-verbal games initiated by the OLD MAN and responded to by PIG, SISSY and MEGA HACKER.

PROCESS: This material was selected from a series of improvisations.

OLD MAN chases PIG, SISSY and MEGA HACKER

OLD MAN spins with his bags in his hands.

OLD MAN extends his hands to PIG, SISSY and MEGA HACKER. They join hands and twist and turn under and through each other's arms.

OLD MAN dives onto the bed. PIG and MEGA HACKER dive under the bed.

SISSY dives underneath the OLD MAN's face. They hold eye contact.

OLD MAN slides off the bed and crawls along the floor.

PIG follows him.

CHAPTER 2. They discover each other.

There are a series of short, interchanging duets. They explore each other's bodies, gently, playfully, boisterously – as if touching someone for the first time. As if their bodies are magnets that are drawing each other in. There is chemistry, but it's not sexual.

PROCESS: made using a game 'over/under'. A goes OVER B's body somehow (A puts his hand on B's shoulder). B goes OVER A's body somehow (B puts her hand on A's hand). A goes UNDER B somehow (B takes her other hand from underneath and lifts it) B goes UNDER A somehow (B turns under A's arm as it comes up).

A goes OVER, B goes OVER, A goes UNDER, B goes UNDER.

DUETS

PIG and OLD MAN

...slides into

PIG and SISSY

...slides into

SISSY and OLD MAN

...slides into

PIG and OLD MAN

OLD MAN lifts and turns MEGA HACKER while PIG and SISSY watch and wait.

They all come together and investigate each other's bodies. Walking their fingers all over each other, examining what they see up close.

CHAPTER 3: THEY DISCOVER THE SPACE. THEY SURRENDER TO THEIR WHIMS.

A rhythm slowly starts to invade – the muffled sound of porn begins and gets gradually louder.

This chapter bursts out across the space. They move quickly between each other. They have short attention spans. Different delights in the space – the props and the set on the stage, each other's bodies – take their full attention for snatched moments.

Their enjoyment of the movement is boisterous and excited.

MEGA HACKER runs to the bed. Stands with her arms outstretched, and falls into PIG's arms.

SISSY stretches across the bed, OLD MAN leans into her feet with his body, and she shoots him off, so that he falls back. PIG catches him as she runs past. MEGA HACKER is lounging, backwards, on the rocking horse. SISSY stands on the bed and stretches upwards like a cat.

OLD MAN starts running around the room. Running for the joy of running. PIG chases him. PIG sees MEGA HACKER and lifts her up. They chase OLD MAN together. SISSY sees the OLD MAN running and chases him too.

PIG and MEGA HACKER move together, PIG lifts and turns and spins HACKER.

OLD MAN and SISSY touch foreheads and turn together.

PIG steals SISSY from OLD MAN. OLD MAN stretches out on some tins of Sex. Stretching like a cat. MEGA HACKER hangs from the bars like a monkey.

PIG pushes SISSY's forehead lightly, so she falls back. PIG catches her, and they take a few steps together. They stand up facing the same way, fold downwards together into a hug, shoot up and back with SISSY kicking her legs into the air. PIG lies backwards over SISSY's back and slides off and rolls away. Like syrup off a spoon. SISSY lies and stretches like a cat.

PIG goes to the bed and stretches into the air, slowly, like a cat.

MEGA HACKER grabs OLD MAN and pushes him to the ground, front down. She lies on top of him. SISSY sees and lies on top of them both. They roll together.

They find PIG.

CHAPTER 4: THEY TRY TO BECOME ONE BODY

Sound – all that is there is the muffled and rhythmic sounds of porn, becoming louder and clearer.

This next chapter is a quartet. They breathe audibly and frantically together. They can feel that this little moment of pure body, pure improvisation, pure sensation delight is slipping away from them.

They join hands and twist and turn under and through each other's arms. An undulating sea of elbows and arms and necks. Getting quicker. Every so often they untangle and arrive in a perfect circle again – but immediately tangle themselves together again. Like they are trying to get inside each other's bodies, or become one body.

As they do this, the next scene (6.) starts to invade.

LITTLE BOY walks on and stands on the bed. He starts snogging a teddy bear and then rubbing it against his crotch.

In the tangle of bodies, OLD MAN becomes unconnected. He goes over to the rocking horse and climbs on. He puts the reins between his teeth and rocks.

SISSY, PIG and MEGA HACKER are trying to keep the tangle of bodies going, but they keep coming back to their perfect circle. It is frustrating.

MEGA HACKER becomes unconnected.

She begins 'The Macarena'.

6.

Pornado. A tornado of porn.

This scene is about the ubiquitous, all-pervading world of porn. It invades the stage. It feels like the entire show is spilling out. No pornographic images are used. No simulating or miming of porn acts.

There is loud, pumping music.

MEGA HACKER is talking very fast into the microphone about the Disney princesses. She thinks they're all sluts.

LITTLE BOY is mimicking a 'sexy' woman. He saunters around, stroking himself, locking eyes with the audience, and biting his lip.

OLD MAN continues to rock on the horse with the reins between his teeth.

QUEEN marches in with a trolley of cakes and seductively displays them to the audience

BEAUTIFUL MAN is wearing heels and doing 'The Macarena'.

PIG and SISSY stand on the edge of the stage, watching.

MEGA HACKER starts performing some ballet. She is narrating her movements. She can't do ballet. But she thinks she can.

LITTLE BOY continues to sexy dance.

OLD MAN is lying on the floor and swimming.

QUEEN rubs the cakes all over her body.

BEAUTIFUL MAN body pops.

PIG and SISSY climb to a raised level on
the set. They start to run on the spot,
in time to the heavy beat of the music.
Determined and full of fire.

Everybody turns to look at the audience.
Then.

BEAUTIFUL MAN is punching some
pillows and saying 'Who's your daddy?!'

MEGA HACKER is at the microphone again
and talking much faster now about the
Disney princesses. She is running on the
spot. As if she's on coke.

LITTLE BOY starts rolling around the floor
as if in a giant duvet.

OLD MAN is sitting on the tins of Sex with
his eyes closed and trying to feel what's
around him in the space.

QUEEN is eating up the space and roaring.
It's as if she is the hottest and most
aggressive chilli pepper in the world.

QUEEN is on the rocking horse and
waving a GB flag. She is singing 'Rule
Britannia'.

BEAUTIFUL MAN is at the microphone,
beating up the air, and singing 'I wanna
dance with somebody' by Whitney
Houston.

MEGA HACKER does 'The Macarena'.

LITTLE BOY is doing 'The Macarena' and laughing hysterically.

OLD MAN does 'The Macarena'.

MEGA HACKER is beating up the air whilst making porn noises 'oooh yeah, yeah baby, you like that, harder yeah.'

LITTLE BOY is on the rocking horse, but he keeps slipping off. He is making porn noises 'oooh yeah, yeah baby, you like that, harder yeah.'

QUEEN is rubbing the microphone against her body and enjoying the sensation.

BEAUTIFUL MAN is flexing his muscles for the audience. And then collapsing and crying and muttering 'help me please help me' on repeat.

OLD MAN is dancing like a 'sexy' woman. Locking eyes with the audience. He growls like a man.

A sound approaches from the back of the stage across the auditorium. Something is collapsing or exploding and it's getting closer. It's coming. It's coming. It's –

Black.

WWW.OBERONBOOKS.COM